AVISSON YOUNG ADULT SERIES

Eight
Who Made
A Difference

Pioneer Women in the Arts

Erica Stux

Avisson Press Inc.
Greensboro

First edition
Printed in the United States of America
ISBN 1-888105-37-2

Library of Congress Cataloging-in-Publication Data

Stux, Erica
    Eight who made a difference : pioneer women in the arts / Erica Stux. --1st ed.
    p. cm. -- (Avisson young adult series)
    Includes bibliographical references and index.
    Summary: profiles eight notable women in the arts, including sculptor Louise Nevelson, photojournalist Margaret Bourke-White, and painter Mary Cassatt.
    ISBN 1-888105-37-2 (lib. bdg.)
    1. Women artists--Biography--Juvenile literature. [1. Artists. 2. Women--Biography.] I. Title. II. Series.
NX164.W65S78 1999
700'.92'2--dc21
[b]   98-54250
                                                          CIP
                                                          AC

Contents

Maria Tallchief in 1965
(AP/WideWorld Photos)

Maria Tallchief, Ballerina

The Osage Indian tribe originally lived in what is now Virginia, but after the white man came, they migrated to the lower Missouri River area. As new settlers continued to take over their land, the tribe moved to Kansas, and then to Oklahoma.

Near the end of the 19th century, oil was discovered on tribal land in Oklahoma, and each Osage family received money for their share of the profits of the growing oil industry. Many of them became so wealthy that the men never had to work.

Although Alexander Tall Chief was one of the wealthiest men among the Osage, he also owned several businesses such as a movie theater and a pool hall in the town of Fairfax, Oklahoma. A handsome man who resembled the Indian on the buffalo nickel, he was a widower with three children when Ruth Porter, a small brown-haired woman of Scotch-Irish and Dutch descent, came from Kansas to visit her sister, who was a housekeeper for Alexander's mother. The two fell in love and married, and in due time had three children - a boy named Gerald, and two daughters: Betty Marie, born January 24, 1925, and Marjorie, born 21 months later.

The family spent their summers in Colorado Springs, where Alexander played golf and Betty Marie had her first dancing lessons. Mrs. Tall Chief was a social leader in Fairfax and wanted to give her children the kind of life she had enjoyed when she was young. She filled the house with books and had both girls take piano and dancing lessons. Because Gerald had trouble learning - the result of being kicked by a horse at age four - it became important to Mrs. Tall Chief that her daughters should be successful.

At five, Betty Marie started attending Sacred Heart Catholic School. Because she could already read, she was placed two grades ahead. Though she loved being outdoors, schoolwork, music and ballet took up most of every day.

The children's Indian grandmother, Eliza Tall Chief, told them stories of how the Osage used to hunt buffalo and have celebrations in their round house made of a wooden framework covered with buffalo skins. Their ceremonies were now forbidden by the U.S. government, but were still held in secret. Because the grandmother wanted the children to learn the Indian traditions, she took them to the ceremonial dances. Betty Marie listened with excitement to the steady beat of the drums, the swishing sound of the gourd rattles filled with pebbles, and the bells sewed onto the leggings of the dancers, whose faces were painted in bright colors.

Mrs. Tall Chief ultimately became dissatisfied with life in Fairfax. To her, the city of Los Angeles held more promise, so in 1933 the family headed for California in their car. Gerald had been sent away to military academy by that time.

The girls were enrolled in piano lessons and in Ernest Belcher's dancing school, where Mr. Belcher made them unlearn everything they had been taught so far. He made them do exercises to strengthen their leg muscles. With her long dark hair pinned up on her head, Betty Marie lifted her legs to the barre until they ached. When she and her sister were considered ready, they took part in a dance recital. They were to do an Indian dance - but the twirling and leaping they were supposed to do was like no Indian dance they had ever seen. Even the drum beats didn't sound Indian!

After four years, the girls switched to another dance studio, headed by Madame Bronislava Nijinska, a small gray-haired woman whose brother was the famous Russian dancer Nijinsky. She worked them hard, correcting their movements until they did them perfectly. "You look like spaghetti!" she would tell a haphazard student in her broken English.

Betty Marie was thrilled when famous dancers that she worshiped from afar visited the studio. One of these, Ada Broadbent, had Betty Marie and Marjorie dance in several of her stage shows in the Los Angeles area.

During Betty Marie's years at Beverly Hills High School, there was no time for school activities or hanging out with friends. In the morning before school she practiced her dance exercises and her piano pieces. After school she practiced again, and at 5 p.m. she and Marjorie had their ballet class lasting two hours. This lesson was the high point of Betty Marie's day. She realized that dancing was what she wanted to do with her life. But she would have to exert herself to reach her goal.

"Dancing must be understood by the head," Madame Nijinska told her, " but it must be felt with the heart. Otherwise you are only a puppet. Let the music speak to you."

At 15, Betty Marie was given a solo part in a ballet based on the music of Chopin, to be performed in the Hollywood Bowl, a huge amphitheater. She hoped to justify Madame

Nijinska's faith in her. Everything went well at the performance until one horrible moment when she slipped and almost fell. She finished the dance, but was almost in tears. Madame Nijinska comforted her, saying it happens to many dancers.

Mrs. Tall Chief insisted that her girls finish high school before moving into careers. Betty Marie had auditioned with the manager of the prestigious Ballet Russe when he was in Los Angeles. He had told her she could join his company while continuing her training. So after graduation, she moved to New York - sad to leave her piano but happy to devote herself totally to dancing.

In New York, she stayed at the home of David Lichine, one of her former dancing teachers. Every day she went to the office of Mr. Denham, the manager, only to be told he was too busy to see her. She became very anxious. The company was going on tour soon. If nothing happened by that time, she would have to return home.

At last she was called in to see Mr. Denham and told she could go on the Canadian tour and would advance if she did well. Happily she wrote her mother, "My dreams are about to come true, and I'm sorry if I'm not fulfilling your dreams for me of becoming a concert pianist."

The U.S. was then (1942) fighting World War II, and Betty Marie realized she was just a wartime replacement, since the foreign-born dancers were not allowed to cross national borders. She would have to work hard to convince the company to keep her.

The girls had long hours of rehearsals, quick meals, and little rest. But Betty Marie learned new dances quickly and could fill in for any of the others. Often she never knew until the last minute which part she was to dance.

At the end of the tour, Mr. Denham offered her a year's contract. Also, he told her she needed a stage name. "But I don't want my last name changed," she protested. They agreed to combine it into one word, and change her first name to Maria. So now she was Maria Tallchief, ballet dancer.

Solo parts were still denied her. She became depressed, stopped eating properly, and grew thinner.

On the next tour, Maria was told she could dance a solo part in a ballet titled Chopin Concerto the following night. Her heart leaped in happiness. But that evening, after putting on her costume and makeup, Mr. Denham told her she was not needed. Someone had thought she was not ready to dance that role. Sadly she stumbled to the dressing room and removed her costume.

But soon a chance came to prove herself. The star ballerina stormed out after an argument with Mr. Denham, and Maria took her place in Chopin Concerto. "I'll show them," she vowed. She finished the dance to thunderous applause. She had proven she was a great dancer. Back in New York, she danced the same role time and again, being now the star of Chopin Concerto. Newspaper reporters wrote about Maria, the Osage Indian Princess. "How silly," she thought; "I want to be known as a great dancer, not as an Indian dancer."

Because most of a dancer's salary went for room and board while on tour, the girls who were not soloists saved money by sharing a room; one slept on the mattress, one on the box springs, and one on the floor. Once Maria overslept and the train left without her for the next stop on the tour. She was frantic. Then she remembered that the next performance was in Columbus, Ohio. A later train allowed her to catch up with the troupe.

The Russian dancers in the company were unfriendly to the American ones, and when Maria was chosen for solo parts, they became downright jealous. However, one male dancer named Sasha befriended her, and they started eating their meals together. Ordinary dating was impossible with their schedules.

In 1944, the Ballet Russe provided dancers for a show titled *Song of Norway*, based on the life and music of the Norwegian composer Edvard Grieg. A blond girl in the chorus set her sights on Sasha. Soon he told Maria he was in love with the other girl. Maria was heartbroken. But in time she got over him.

The great choreographer George Balanchine joined the company in 1944 as its dance director. Maria was impressed with the way he made the dance steps fit the music. He had a way of inspiring his dancers, and Maria enjoyed working with him. Balanchine created a new dance just for Maria, based on a Hans Christian Anderson story "The Ice Maiden". It became a smash hit, the critics praised it, and people flocked to the theater to see Maria in it.

Balanchine gave Maria more and more important roles. Her dancing capabilities improved "beyond anything I'd ever imagined," she wrote. "My body seemed to be going through a metamorphosis."

Personal relations between Maria and Balanchine were rather formal. Therefore she was astounded when he proposed marriage. She knew she wanted to dance for him . . . but marry him? It seemed too fantastic!

Upon reflection, she realized the idea was not so far-fetched. George personified her passions - music and dance. Why shouldn't she spend the rest of her life with him?

"But he's a foreigner!" Maria's mother wailed when given the news. "And twenty years older than you!"

Nevertheless, Maria and George were married on August 16, 1946, in New York. She understood that their public life would take precedence over their private life. She was his wife, but - perhaps more important - she was his ballerina.

Balanchine had left the Ballet Russe the year before and formed his own company. Although the Ballet Russe wanted to keep Maria and had bestowed on her the coveted title of Ballerina, she felt she had to go with Balanchine. When he became dance director of the Paris Opera, she joined him in France. The proud French thought that no American could be good enough to dance at their opera. However, they were overcome with awe; Maria was definitely as good or better than any French dancer.

Before leaving Paris, Maria and George attended her sister Marjorie's wedding. Marjorie had also become a ballet dancer, and both she and her fiance were in France with the Marquis de Cuevas Ballet.

In New York, Balanchine created another role for Maria - one that would make her shine like nothing before. On November 27, 1949, Maria danced in the first performance of *The Firebird*, a story based on a Russian folktale. This was to be the high point of Maria's career, her husband told her.

The audience was entranced as she made her entrance in great flying leaps. Sequins on her costume, red slippers, and tall red plumes on her head transformed her into *The Firebird.* The newspaper critics marveled. Everyone in New York felt they had to see this ballet. But on tour in Europe, audiences did not care for it; it was too strange and overpowering to them. To Maria, it seemed that they rejected her as well as the ballet.

Balanchine also rejected her, having fallen in love with another dancer even younger than Maria. But it was all right with Maria because she was seeing a young airline pilot named Elmourza while the company was in London. Balanchine had loved her, his third wife, more as a dancer than as a woman. They agreed to separate after the London tour. In a way the separation was a relief to Maria;

14

she no longer had to be perfect onstage as Balanchine's chosen ballerina.

Maria was given a new dancing partner, Andre Eglevsky, who was already well-known worldwide. He had a way of bringing out the best from his partners. The two had an extremely successful tour of Europe. They also danced in live performances for the then-popular variety shows on TV.

Maria and Elmourza were married in October 1952. However, he had no interest in ballet and no idea how much dancing meant to Maria. She had no choice but to divorce him after less than two years. This move left her sad and empty, but she managed to rise above her sadness. She was now a stronger, finer person, and this was reflected in her dancing.

Recognized as a true artist, not only a dancer, Maria's picture and interviews appeared in popular magazines. This fame filled her with both pride and humility.

Another man came into Maria's life, a Chicago businessman named Henry "Buzz" Paschen. He began flying from Chicago to New York every weekend to be with Maria. After a year's courtship, in June 1956, the two got married in Chicago. Immediately after the wedding, Maria flew to New York to continue her career. Retirement for her was unthinkable; she was now in her prime as a dancer.

In January 1959, Maria gave birth to a baby girl, who was named Elise Marie. Maria returned to dancing as soon as possible. She was still associated with George Balanchine, who cast her in many of his dance creations. She had to admit to herself that her career was more fulfilling than her marriage. But she declined to go on long tours that would take her away from her baby.

In 1966 Maria hung up her ballet slippers for good and settled in Chicago with her husband. From then on she devoted herself to teaching dance, working with the Chicago Indian Center, and participating in Indian cultural studies at various universities.

Many honors came to Maria during her career. The people of Oklahoma were especially proud of her. The Osage tribe had a special ceremony in which she was given an "honor name" that meant "Woman of Two Standards," or woman who had brought honor to both the Osage people and the American people as a whole. An Indian song composed just for her was sung. Maria was touched; pride surged within her, to be able to represent the Osage people to the entire world.

The Washington Press Club twice named Maria "Woman of the Year," and the Oklahoma Hall of Fame placed her among its members. Leaders of foreign countries invited her to dinner whenever she danced in their capital cities. In 1996 she was among those honored at the Kennedy Center for their contribution to the arts.

Maria Tallchief will be remembered for putting American ballet on an equal footing with that of European countries, where ballet first developed.

Louise Nevelson in 1971
(AP/WideWorld Photos)

Louise Nevelson, Sculptor

Louise Nevelson always regarded her life as following a pre-ordained blueprint—a ready-made plan that unrolled as she grew and which she followed without thinking about it.

She was born in the city of Kiev, then part of Russia, in late 1899, the second child and oldest girl of Isaac and Minna Berliawsky. When Louise was two, her father left for the United States, as many young Jewish men did in order to avoid religious persecution and service in the Russian army.

Louise was traumatized by her father's departure, and for six months refused to speak. After three years in the U.S., Isaac sent money for his family to join him. Minna packed up her three children and her best belongings and began the journey by horse-drawn wagon, train, and steamship. Their ship arrived in March 1905, and they joined Isaac in the town of Rockland, Maine, where he had found work as a woodcutter and a quarry laborer. Later he went into business as a junk dealer, lumber dealer, and real estate broker.

Rockland had been a prosperous ship-building

town, surrounded by dark pine trees and white birches, but by 1900 industry had shifted to mining limestone and smelting it into usable forms. Wealthy families came to Rockland in the summer to vacation in luxury hotels. The town's social life centered around its churches. There was a general uneasiness about foreign newcomers, and the thirty or so Jewish families were aware of a subtle antagonism.

Mrs. Berliawsky took pleasure in dressing herself and her daughters in expensive, stylish clothes, such as Persian lamb coats and hats. Though at times it was embarrassing, Louise absorbed the idea that such extravagance was a form of self-expression.

By the time she was six, Louise was assembling and carving scraps of wood from her father's lumber yeard. A shy and self-conscious child, she was known as "the artist" at school. When a librarian asked the pretty nine-year-old with a big white bow in her dark hair what she wanted to be, she replied immediately " an artist — a sculptor." The clue to understanding her as a child, she wrote later, was "the irony of a terribly shy person who is absolutely sure of herself."

At Rockland High School, Louise was only an average student, but excelled at sports. Being the tallest girl in the ninth grade led to her election as captain of the school basketball team, an honor she was too shy to refuse. She had few friends in school, but this did not bother her. She had her own fantasies and her own view of her destiny.

Louise planned after high school to move to New York and study art. But a detour in her plans arrived in the form of Charles Nevelson. He was in his family's shipping business, and the Nevelsons of New York represented wealth, power, and culture to Louise. She and Charles were married in 1920, and after wedding trips to New Orleans and Cuba, where Charles had shipping business, they settled into an apartment in New York City.

Life in New York consisted of evenings at nightclubs or lectures or the theater, luncheons or teas with women friends, business trips with Charles, and chauffeured car trips to her family in Maine. Louise was at first entranced with this life, but unsure how to use her abundant energy and imagination.

Looking back many years later, she wrote "Marriage was the only complication in my life... I learned that marriage wasn't the romance that I sought but a partnership, and I didn't need a partner."

In searching for her own identity, Louise

explored various avenues of creativity through lessons in modern dance, painting, voice, and dramatics. Marriage felt oppressive to her. The birth of her son Myron, nicknamed Mike, increased this feeling. "I don't think I gave him any particular attention," she admitted later. "I didn't understand what being a mother meant."

Luckily for the baby, there were nannies to care for him. But Louise's feelings of inadequacy led to tremendous guilt.

In explaining her development as an artist, she stated, "It was only because I had so little confidence in the world that I wanted to build my own world . . . Sometimes one has to spend time in an anti-world to become conscious, free, and powerful in the chosen one."

The shipping business took a downward turn. Louise, Charles, and the baby moved into smaller quarters. Louise began to dress in flamboyant outfits that embarrassed her husband. She was a beautiful woman who commanded attention, and Charles, afraid of losing her, became possessive and argumentative. Her in-laws criticized her, and suggested she was socially and culturally inferior to them. There was a continual conflict between her own needs and those of her husband and son. "Within the Nevelson circle, you could know

Beethoven, but God forbid if you were Beethoven," she wrote.

A visit to a display of kimonos worn by actors in the classical Japanese theater gave Louise a new inner vision and drive to create something of beauty. She began full-time study at the Art Students League in 1929, and found happiness there. The League's sense of community among its students gave Louise the confidence she needed. She developed her gift of looking at ordinary objects in an unconventional way. Where others would see only a building with many windows, Louise, like a true artist, saw reflections that changed as the sun moved, and patterns in the bricks or the supporting columns.

The ideas concerning art of a German painter named Hans Hofmann spread to the Art Students League. Louise detemined that she had to go to Germany to study with him. The Berliawsky family put up the money to finance her trip.

After three months with Hofmann, Louise took to traveling around Europe. She got bit parts in a few movies shot in Munich and in Vienna, and she discovered Pablo Picasso's art, which featured cubes and other geometrical figures. "When I found cubism, it was like when some people find God, and I have never left it," Louise recalled years later.

She had now separated from Charles, although they were not legally divorced until 1941. "I gave myself the greatest gift I could have, my own life," she said. A second trip to Europe in 1932 left her disappointed. She realized that the vitality of America offered the most inspiration to an artist. "I could be a leaf on a tree in Paris," she wrote, "but I could be that tree in America."

A friend introduced Louise to the great Mexican artist Diego Rivera, then in New York, who painted large socialist-oriented murals. She became one of Rivera's assistants, copying small sketches onto a large mural.

In the meantime she also created her own sculptures and drawings. She always worked quickly, having the completed product in her mind's eye. For Louise, there was no interval between the idea and the product.

Various New York galleries showed her work during the 1930s. Her sculptures from this period were of female figures, either running or dancing. More and more she was drawn to sculpture, because, as she put it, her "physical energy wanted to push something into shape." The New York Times described one exhibit as "unlike anything we've ever seen before....They are small wood sculptures conceived abstractly and with special concern for the tensions of planes and volumes. But they are coated with multi-colored paints. For example, one arm of a figure is painted blue and another yellow.... She uses (color) plastically and structurally to emphasize some planes and de-emphasize others, to increase the volume of a certain section as it stands in relationship to another."

This assessment of her work did much to increase Louise's self-confidence, but she had periods of depression worrying about her son, her finances, health, and struggle for recognition. She sold her jewelry to raise money, but by the late 1930s it was gone. Her brother Nate sent her money occasionally, and a number of male admirers bought her beautiful clothes. American museums in the late 1930s were beginning to acquire works of American women artists, but Louise was not among them. She was hurt and angry. Then, as World War II broke out, many European artists arrived in New York as exiles from their own countries. Although these artists felt themselves superior to the Americans, Louise felt stimulated by exposure to the Europeans' paintings and sculptures.

When she felt the time had come to show the world what she had created, she asked the most important art dealer in New York, Karl Nierendorf, to come to her studio. Impressed with her work, he gave her a one-woman exhibition. The art critics gave her kind reviews, but none of her pieces were sold.

In the 1940s, American art was in an experimental stage. With no market for artistic output, artists were free to keep experimenting and growing. Early recognition of individual artists would only have inhibited the evolution of their work.

Louise Nevelson kept experimenting also— with metal, fabric, clay, marble, and mixed media. But mostly she preferred working with wood, which she considered a feminine medium. She collected wood scraps wherever she could. Often she pushed a wheelbarrow through the streets at 3 or 4 a.m., to beat the garbage trucks that would pick up discarded items later. During this period, her wood creations were painted black, because "black creates harmony and doesn't intrude on the emotions." She also made a series of etchings at this time.

After her mother's death in 1943, Louise felt the need for a decent home, and purchased a house on East 30th Street. It had a large garden area, where she could work eight months of the year. The spacious rooms were hung with paintings and divided into areas by her sculptures. At times her brother and one sister came to live with her. Louise's son Mike was now away at sea, serving in the merchant marine. Eventually he turned to sculpture, too.

The death of her mentor Nierendorf in 1948 left Louise dejected. Her house became the scene for weekly discussions among leading artists. For a number of years, she seldom exhibited, but she was far from idle. Her work now consisted of entire assemblages of wooden pieces related in some way. An exhibition called Royal Voyage consisted of sculptures symbolizing kings, queens, and things of the sea, all of them covered with black paint. This was one of the first exhibits whose pieces united to create a mood , an entire environment. Her method of work was to paint each piece of wood first, then combine them instinctively into units and then into entire walls. "I never knew my next move," Louise told a reporter. "I just let it happen. When I let my inner vision guide my hands, there are no errors."

She made an effort to be seen in all the right places—nightclubs as well as art shows—to further her career and reputation. No place was too obscure or out of the way to show her work. In the 1950s Louise exhibited sculptures, drawings, and paintings in about 60 shows. "You move up a little and get pulled down, and so it goes," she wrote to her son. Gradually her sculptures began to win prizes, and her name appeared more often in the art press.

Moon Garden Plus One was a 1958 exhibit of interconnected or interrelated wood sculptures marked by repeated vertical lines of varying height, and an abundance of detail. Part of this exhibit was a unit called Sky Cathedral, probably one of Louise's greatest works. A blue light in the gallery cast shadows that further intensified this mini-environment. "Her shadowy facades are inexhaustibly complex, affording endless explorations to the eye," wrote an art critic.

Moon Garden Plus One gave Louise recognition, but art collectors found it impossible to purchase any individual pieces because they were so huge and because in separating them from the collection, the total effect was lost. However, a New York art dealer offered her a steady income in exchange for sculptures to be sold, and also promoted her work in Europe. At last Louise's financial problems seemed to be ended.

Because museum directors had long ignored her, Louise harbored great bitterness toward them. When one director arrived ten minutes late for an appointment at her studio and apologized, she responded, "What's ten minutes? Where were you ten years ago?"

Not only in her art, but also in her personal appearance, Louise Nevelson emerged as a unique public figure. Because she always felt intensely feminine, she never wore slacks. Her wardrobe was a synthesis of unusual fabrics. One of her favorite ensembles was a skirt made from a Pennsylvania Dutch patchwork quilt worn under a Chinese imperial robe, the whole overlaid by a floor-length Persian coat of brightly-colored paisley. In her later years, she took to wearing a scarf or other headdress over her thinning gray hair, and thick eyelashes. She felt more at ease when she created a striking image. When in her seventies, the clothing designer Arnold Scaasi invited her to his workshop and began showing her tailored suits, which she rejected.

" You are right," he said. "We must dress you as the empress of art." With Louise's suggestions, he created lavish, attention-getting clothes for her that made her feel like the beautiful woman she once was.

A major figure in the American world of art by the late 1950s, Louise lacked only a museum exhibition. In 1959, Dorothy Miller, curator of the

Museum of Modern Art, asked Louise to be part of an exhibition titled Sixteen Americans. For three months, Louise assembled her pieces—all-white columnar units, boxes, and free-standing objects, the whole called Dawn's Wedding Feast. She hoped that someone would purchase the entire "environment", but this did not happen. Some single pieces were sold. The others were returned to her studio, to re-emerge years later as parts of other "environments".

In 1962 Louise was invited to exhibit in the Venice Biennale, the most prestigious of international art exhibitions. An exhibit of Nevelson works was at that time making the rounds of various European museums. It was detoured to Venice and installed in three rooms of the American Pavilion. To enhance the mood of the exhibit, Louise had the circular entrance room painted gold, another room white, and the third one black.

The prestige of participating in the Venice exhibition led to an offer to join the Sidney Janis gallery, which represented some of the leading American artists. But the financial success Louise expected did not materialize. She ended up owing Sidney Janis money spent to prepare her show at his gallery. Even though she raised money by selling her house, she was broke, depressed, and angry.

Deliverance came in the form of an invitation to Los Angeles to produce a series of prints at the Tamarind Lithography Workshop, all expenses paid. Louise immersed herself in this work, producing prints that, she was told, were valued at $150,000. The rest of her anger and depression disappeared with that knowledge.

By 1966 museums and private collectors were eagerly buying Louise Nevelson's output. The prices of her works jumped. "I enjoy the fact that a woman artist in America can collect wooden scraps from the street, put them together, and sell them to the Rockefellers for $100,000," she remarked.

Late in life, Louise turned to metal sculpture, perhaps because of its greater permanence than wood. She also worked with plexiglass, then abandoned it after two years, feeling she had done all she could in that medium without repeating herself.

On a visit to a machine shop where her steel sculptures were being manufactured, Louise found and took home a load of aluminum scraps. These became the basis of a new series of sculptures titled Seventh Decade Garden. They are tall undulating creations, each curved piece laid flat against the others, the whole flaring outward near the top like a bouquet.

Through the 1970s, commissions poured in to create large sculptures for public buildings or for outdoors. For an outdoor sculpture, Louise first studied where it was to be placed. To her, "the artist must be aware of where they are placed and what is around them, because everything will alter the piece by interaction." The changing quality of light, the climate, and the landscape all affected the size and form of her creations. These commissions gave Louise the incentive to keep creating. "I have so much to do, I don't have time to die," she remarked when in her seventies.

New York gave Louise a huge party for her 80th birthday. She was deluged with awards and honorary degrees from universities, and President Ronald Reagan presented her with a National Medal of the Arts. Though it was not in her nature to feel grateful to anyone, her old bitterness subsided.

"Art gives me my world, it gives me my sanity, it gives me my beauty, and it gives me my life," Louise stated in a speech.

Louise Nevelson died in April 1988 in New York City. Through her long professional life, she was an integral part of 20th century sculpture. She was responsible for the renewal of sculpture as a branch of American art, and extended sculpture into the realm of illusion.

Marian Anderson performing at the Lincoln Memorial before a crowd of 75,000 spectators, Easter Sunday 1939
(AP/Wide World Photos)

Marian Anderson, Singer

Marian Anderson was born in Philadelphia on February 17, 1899, the oldest of three girls. Her father worked at the Reading Terminal Market and her mother, who had been a school teacher in Virginia before marrying, took in laundry for extra money. Singing was a common occurrence in the family. Mr. Anderson might croon snatches of "Asleep in the Deep" while dressing, and Mrs. Anderson often sang spirituals while doing her housework. Some evenings, when the weather didn't allow sitting outside on the steps, Mrs. Anderson and the girls would sing hymns or folksongs for their own amusement. Prayer was also important in the Anderson home. The girls were taught to say their prayers each evening, and this became a lifelong habit.

One of Marian's earliest pleasures was the family's yearly trip to see the circus. Each of the girls would have a new outfit to wear. A large basket of food was taken along on the trolley ride. "Our eyes were wide with delight, trying to follow all the acts going on at the same time under the big tent," Marian wrote in her autobiography.

Shortly after her sixth birthday, Marian was asked to join the junior choir at church. When she was eight, the family acquired a piano. Marian fingered the keys lovingly. There was not enough money for piano lessons, but Marian and her sisters managed to pick out a few melodies. Once, while delivering a basket of laundry for her mother, she saw a black lady through a window making beautiful music come from a piano. Some day, she thought, maybe I can make music like that.

She earned money, a few pennies at a time, by scrubbing the steps of neighbors' houses and running errands. Her heart was set on buying a violin hanging in the window of a pawnshop. When her savings reached the grand sum of four dollars, she bought it and proudly brought it home. A family friend showed her how to tune it and how to place her fingers on the strings. But gradually the strings broke, one after another, and the violin became unplayable. That was the end of Marian's career as a violinist.

On some Sundays Marian was allowed to sing a solo or duet at church services. Once she took part in a benefit concert to raise money for a new church. "Come and hear the baby contralto, ten years old" the handbills announced. She was really only eight.

Mr. Anderson died while his girls were still young. Marian sensed that their lives were about to change. The family moved in with Mr. Anderson's parents, and Mrs. Anderson went to work every day, doing cleaning and laundry, since her teaching license was no good in Philadelphia. Besides the three Anderson girls, an aunt and two cousins also lived there, and Grandmother Anderson kept two or three other children whose mothers could not care for them. Marian's mother did her share of the housekeeping and contributed to the rent. Money was always in short supply, but nobody complained.

At thirteen, Marian was invited to join the church's adult choir. She could sing in any register, high like a soprano or low like an alto or tenor, so if anyone was absent, she could fill in and sing that part. "I became convinced that my presence in the senior and junior choirs was not only a duty but a necessity for the church and me, and I never missed a Sunday," she wrote. "The congregation made me feel that I was an indispensable part of what went on there. It was a stimulating experience."

Visitors at the Union Baptist Church invited

the choir to come and sing at their own churches. If it was too far away or too expensive to send the whole group, two or four might be sent, and of course Marian was always included. She could now play simple accompaniments on the piano while she sang. Regular piano lessons were still beyond the family's finances.

When Marian was a fourteen-year-old, neighbors advised Mrs. Anderson, " Let Marian go out and work, she's a big girl now." But Mrs. Anderson wouldn't hear of it. At William Penn High School, Marian enrolled in business classes so that she could get a job as soon as possible and contribute her earnings to the family. But her heart was not in typing or shorthand; she was happiest in the weekly music class. She sang in the school chorus and occasionally got solos. Once a visitor heard her sing in a school assembly, and told the principal, "This girl should be in a college prep course and do as much as possible with music." Marian transferred to South Philadelphia High School, where the principal took a personal interest in her.

A noted tenor appearing as guest artist at the church's annual gala concert also took an interest in Marian and recommended professional studies. The church took up a special collection one Sunday to pay for whatever Marian needed. The total collected was $17.02. What she needed most were new shoes and a dress for special occasions. Rather than buying a ready-made dress, she purchased material and sewed one with her mother's help. It cost less than ten dollars, and she got many compliments on it. She could not put into words how grateful she felt toward the good people of her church.

The more Marian sang in church, the more she was asked to sing in other places. Some afternoons she rushed home from school, did her household chores and homework, and hurried to the YWCA or the Methodist or Episcopal Church to fulfill an engagement. Sometimes there were two or even three engagements the same evening. Payment was usually one or two dollars, which she gave to her mother. Eventually she set her fee at five dollars. Her only expense was the streetcar fare. An officer of the Philadelphia Choral Society told Mrs. Anderson, "One of these days, your daughter will earn fifty dollars a night." It was only a few years before his prediction came true.

Out-of-town engagements kept Marian from school occasionally, for several days at a time. When she attended regularly, days went by without learning anything new, "but just let me stay away a couple of days, and the class had gone wild learning new things. My teachers were understanding . . . They would assign extra lessons and give me make-up examinations."

Up to now, Marian sang naturally, just as the music made her feel. But she realized she needed training. She was put in touch with a black lady, Mary Patterson, who agreed to give her free lessons. Mrs. Patterson taught her to throw her voice into a corner of the ceiling - a more controlled way of singing.

In addition, Marian went to enroll in a music school in Philadelphia. When she asked for an application, she was turned away with the cold statement: "We don't take colored." She felt like a bucket of ice water had been dumped on her. This was something she had never encountered— not at school nor in her mixed neighborhood.

On train trips to sing in other cities, she also experienced discrimination. Either she was told no reservations were available, or she was placed in the coach behind the locomotive, where ventilation was poor and riders would get a faceful of smoke and soot from an open window.

Marian acquired an accompanist, a young man named Billy King, and a new voice teacher, Giuseppe Boghetti, who told her, "After two years with me, you will be ready to sing anywhere." Money was still a problem. The Union Baptist Church arranged a benefit concert, which raised $600. Mr. Boghetti gave Marian voice exercises and worked on her breathing and the unevenness of her tones. She learned songs by Schubert, Brahms, Schumann and Rachmaninoff; Russian songs, Italian and French songs, and of course songs in English. At her weekly lesson, "you always wished you could invent some way to hold back the clock ..... If another pupil happened not to turn up, Mr. Boghetti let you stay on, and those extra minutes you cherished and remembered."

When the $600 was exhausted, Mr. Boghetti kept her on without payment for a year. In time she repaid him fully. At recitals in his studio, "he would sit in one of the front rows and fix his eyes squarely on yours while you were singing. Somehow he helped you sing better than you thought you could."

Billy King became Marian's manager as well as her accompanist. They appeared in churches, college auditoriums, and theaters rented by local promoters. Being booked into theaters gave her a deep sense of accomplishment. Her fee rose to $50, then $100. Out of this came their train fare, $25 for Billy's accompanying and something additional for his management.

Marian now felt that with continued study there was no limit to what she could do with her voice. Her audiences were no longer exclusively black people. She was ready, she thought, for a recital in New York's prestigious Town Hall. The hall was rented, flyers were printed and distributed, and Mr. Boghetti had her learn four new songs. But the audience was very small and the newspaper critics were not kind. Marian returned to Philadelphia defeated, her hopes dashed.

"Listen," her mother said, "whatever you do in this world, no matter how good it is, you will never be able to please everybody. All you can strive for is to do the best it is humanly possible for you to do."

By this time, Mrs. Anderson and the girls were living in their own house. They acquired items they had long dreamed of having, like a radio-phonograph, and it was easier to have friends over for dinner. A young man Marian had met when singing in Wilmington started calling at the Anderson house. His name was Orpheus H. Fisher, nicknamed King, and he was attending art school in Philadelphia. He became very fond of Marian, and she returned his affection. But when he proposed marriage, she turned him down.

"I'm too busy building up my career," she told

him. " I travel a lot, and that wouldn't be fair to you. I just can't consider marriage right now." However, the two stayed in touch, and eventually married in 1943.

Before long, Marian began visiting Mr. Boghetti's studio again. She needed to earn money so that her family could buy furniture for their new house. Mr. Boghetti found a language coach for Marian, because the German repertory in particular gave her trouble. It is important for a singer to get foreign pronunciations right and to understand exactly what she is singing. Then Mr. Boghetti entered her in competitions. She had no trouble winning one in Philadelphia. An important one in New York drew 300 contestants. The semi-finalists were announced; Marian was among them. Then a phone call came to Mr. Boghetti's studio. Marian had won!

The prize was an appearance at the Lewisohn Stadium with the New York Philharmonic Orchestra. The concert took place August 26, 1925. The *New York Times* wrote, "Miss Anderson made an excellent impression. She is endowed by nature with a voice of unusual compass, color, and dramatic capacity . . ."

Marian now moved into the major league of singers. Invitations to sing came from Canada and the west coast, as well as from the eastern states. Several concert series included Marian as one attraction. Her fee went up to $350, and $500 in special places. She purchased additional evening dresses for her appearances, for she realized that black people would feel good seeing one of their own well-dressed. She also began studies with a new teacher in New York, traveling weekly from Philadelphia for a one-hour lesson. Frank La Forge was a kind, thoughtful man, and Marian benefited immensely from her one year of lessons with him.

Before long, Marian realized her progress was at a standstill. She needed to go to Europe, and so she spent one year in London with new voice teachers. But then her money ran low. She missed her family and friends, so she returned home feeling she hadn't accomplished much.

The following year, a six-month grant took Marian to Germany and another voice coach. Since a concert in Berlin seemed important, she put up $500 of her own for the arrangements.

The German audience was sure to be critical. Though at first nervous, she felt the audience becoming receptive after several songs, perhaps even enthusiastic. Next morning, she scanned the newspapers eagerly, looking for reviews. There was nothing. Didn't they think she was worthy of a review? It turned out that the newspapers were very slow in printing reviews. When they did appear about a week later, they were complimentary towards Marian.

Another grant, in 1933, allowed Marian to return to Europe. This time she stayed two years, and performed in almost every town in Sweden, Denmark, Norway, and Finland. The Scandinavian people came out of curiosity; they had never seen a black performer before. One newspaper described her as being "dressed in electric blue satin and looking very much like a chocolate bar." The reporter did not mean to be unkind; he merely expressed his wonder. The initial curiosity toward her subsided quickly. Strangers came to her hotel room, others sent flowers, and people followed her on the street and smiled in the most friendly way. Marian was happy to be accepted there as a human being and an artist.

Some of the Scandinavian audiences were warm and responsive, others less so. Marian's Finnish accompanist arranged for her to meet the great Finnish composer Jan Sibelius, then about 70 years old. After she sang for him, he rose to embrace her. She was deeply touched.

Appearances in London and Paris followed, and then Vienna. To be accepted in Vienna—the city of

Schubert and Beethoven—would be a milestone. At Marian's Viennese concert, she held the audience enthralled. In Salzburg, the great conductor Arturo Toscanini came backstage to congratulate her after a performance. "That is a voice such as one hears only once in a hundred years," was his comment.

On board ship, returning to the U.S., Marian fell and broke her ankle. This made her homecoming concert in New York's Town Hall rather awkward. Her long gown hid the cast on her leg, but how could she walk onstage gracefully? The problem was solved by using a wheelchair and keeping the curtain closed until she was in place.

Marian's next tour of Europe included cities in Russia. Here she encountered a strange custom. Audiences rushed to the stage as she finished singing and pounded on it, demanding encores. She was paid in bulky packages of rubles, which she had to spend before leaving the country. Consequently she brought home much jewelry and several fur evening wraps. Marian was now under contract with Sol Hurok, the prime manager of American artists. He wanted her to be accepted as an artist equal to any other. She remained ever thankful to him for his personal interest and deep faith in her.

An unpleasant incident arose in 1938: Marian was refused an appearance at Constitution Hall in Washington, D.C. No blacks had ever performed there, or would ever, according to the hall's owners, the Daughters of the American Revolution. Many important people, among them Eleanor Roosevelt, protested this decision. Then, as though to make up for this snub, an invitation came from the Department of the Interior of the U.S. government to sing in front of the Lincoln Memorial on Easter Sunday, 1939. When Marian walked out to face the audience, she encountered a sea of faces stretching into the distance. She almost choked with emotion as she sang the National Anthem. Soon after that, she sang at the White House when the king and queen of England visited President Roosevelt.

Many of Marian's concerts during the 1930s and 1940s were benefits to raise money for various worthy causes. The Daughters of the American Revolution changed their rules, and Marian sang several times at Constitution Hall, always to sold-out concerts.

During those years, Marian was aware that hotels where she stayed did not normally accept blacks. She always took her meals in her hotel room, to avoid any unpleasantness. In one town, the local manager got upset that Marian took her bows holding the hand of her white accompanist. "We won't stand for that here," the manager told her. She never sang in that town again. Some towns had segregated seating, whites on one side, blacks on the other. Marian decided at one point that she would not sing where this occurred. It led to the loss of several engagements a year, but that was a principle she had to uphold.

From 1935 on, Marian made many recordings. Each of her albums sold at least 250,000 copies. Her "Ave Maria" alone sold 750,000 copies. Spirituals, Christmas carols and Schubert songs were the best-selling collections.

After Marian married Orpheus "King" Fisher in 1943, they bought a farm in Connecticut. She was always happy to get back to this home and to her husband after weeks and months of touring. Her summers were spent there going over her repertory of songs and choosing which ones to use in the coming season. Her programs usually ended with a group of spirituals.

An offer came from the Metropolitan Opera: would Marian Anderson be interested in singing the part of Ulrica in Verdi's opera *The Masked Ball*? At first she wavered, saying the music was too high for her voice. But the opera conductor Dimitri Mitropoulos encouraged her to accept. Now she had to get busy studying the part, and also learning how to act. The performance took place January 7, 1955. It could have gone better, she thought, but everyone seemed satisfied, and the "Met" asked her back for the next season. She knew she was a symbol, the first Negro to sing on that hallowed stage. She took pride in the knowledge that she opened the door for other black singers.

By this time, Marian Anderson was well-known throughout the world, and admired not only for her voice, but for her dignity and courage. In 1957 the U.S. government sent her on a tour to represent her country abroad. She sang in twelve countries of Asia, and covered 40,000 miles. Recognizing her talent for bridging differences among people, President Eisenhower in 1958 appointed Marian as a delegate to the United Nations. In this capacity, she spoke out on many issues, mostly those involving areas of Africa. She earned the respect of all those who came in contact with her.

When her assignment with the U.N. was over, Marian resumed her career. Her last recital took place in 1965 at Carnegie Hall. She then took up a quieter life at her home in Connecticut. On her 75th birthday, she sang Schubert's "Ave Maria" at a benefit concert sponsored by Young Audiences, an organization that introduced young people to classical music. At this concert, she received several awards, one of them the United Nations Peace Prize for her work with the U.N. She had already been awarded the Presidential Medal of Freedom in 1963, and had been named " Woman of the Year" by several organizations. Other honors came: awards from the governments of Sweden, Finland, and Japan, and honorary degrees from over thirty universities. Her career was successful even beyond the wildest of her early dreams.

Marian Anderson died in Portland, Oregon, on April 8, 1993.

**Nadia Boulanger, as the first woman conductor of the Boston
Symphony Orchestra, in 1938.**
(AP/WideWorld Photos)

Nadia Boulanger, Musician and Mentor

Whenever Ernest Boulanger gave a singing lesson in his home, four-year-old Nadia wailed at the first sound of music; and when she and her mother encountered street musicians on walks through their Paris neighborhood, she howled and hid her face in her mother's skirt.

This behavior changed completely a year later, when Madame Boulanger was expecting another child. Perhaps Nadia subconsciously wanted to please her parents by embracing music, and keep them from centering their attention on the new baby. She threw herself eagerly into music lessons, and progressed rapidly.

Madame Boulanger had been a beautiful Russian teenager and aspiring singer named Raissa Myschetsky when she met Ernest Boulanger in St. Petersburg while he was on a concert tour in Russia. The Boulanger family was steeped in music. Ernest's father had been a cello teacher, and his mother, a singer at the Paris Comic Opera. Ernest had studied piano and composition at the

Paris Conservatory of Music, and had a successful career teaching, performing, and composing. He had not married because of a belief that insanity ran in his family, a belief that originated from one cousin's suicide and another cousin's fits of depression.

Raissa, who was to be always evasive about her family background, followed Ernest to Paris and prevailed upon him to let her join his voice classes. Two years later they were married, when she was twenty and he was 62. Their first child died at 15 months. The second was Nadia, born September 16, 1887. Raissa devoted herself single-mindedly to the child's education. She taught Nadia German, Russian, and geography, and pushed her relentlessly to study. She demanded the best from Nadia, yet filled her with humility and self-doubt, which Nadia carried with her throughout her life. Young Nadia was full of pranks and continually rebelled against her mother's firm discipline. When she did well at her lessons, by way of a reward her mother asked her, "Where would you like to go?" giving her a choice of attending a concert or perhaps an outing to one of the parks of Paris.

Nadia was groomed almost from birth to become a breadwinner, to support her family in the future. The reasons were two-fold: there would not be enough money for a dowry (the money that a young lady was supposed to bring with her when she married, according to the custom of the time)— and Madame Boulanger was sure to face many years of widowhood and had no intention of working herself.

When Nadia's sister Lili was born, her father took her to see the new baby and made her promise that she would be responsible for her sister's welfare. It was an emotional experience for a six-year-old. Many years later she said, "I went into that room as a carefree child, and I left it as an adult."

At nine, after two years of private lessons, Nadia was considered ready to take the entrance exam for the prestigious Paris Conservatory of Music. She took her place as the youngest student there in December 1896.

Students remained in a class until they earned a prize in that class's year-end competition. Nadia's mother accompanied her to her classes and quizzed her on the material at home. When Nadia was called on in class to sing a passage, Raissa brushed the bangs from her daughter's forehead so that she could see the music better. Already Nadia had to wear glasses.

Little Lili absorbed the music she heard at

home, and could sing at three what Nadia could do only at six. But she was always a sickly child; she had survived a severe case of pneumonia at three, and was later diagnosed as having Crohn's disease, an incurable condition which periodically sapped her strength.

After Mr. Boulanger died in 1900, it was imperative for Nadia to win a prize at the Conservatory, for only then could she earn money to help support her family. At 13 she took the most difficult course offered: piano accompaniment, which included sight reading, improvising an accompaniment to a given melody, transposing at sight, and playing a full orchestral score on the piano at sight. All these skills had to become second nature to the students.

Finally, at 16, Nadia won all the first prizes she had aimed for, in organ, piano accompaniment, and composition. But her mother would not let her enjoy her success. "You are quite pleased with yourself, aren't you?" she said. " But are you certain that you did all that you could?"

In 1904 Nadia began to teach. Her students were about her own age, but Nadia's serious manner, long black dresses, and hair drawn back from her face made her look older. She also played the organ in public occasionally. All her earnings went to help support her mother and sister, who maintained the appearance of aristocracy; this status, however, was denied to Nadia by virtue of her being a "working girl."

Soon Nadia was in demand as a soloist, accompanist, and teacher. The songs she composed were performed in Paris salons. But a steady job was what she needed. She was given a teaching position at a new school of music, and in 1909 was appointed assistant to a professor at the Paris Conservatory. All this brought in enough to pay her expenses and finance her mother's lavish parties and trips to spas. The previous year Nadia had won the Second Grand Prize in the important Prix de Rome Competition for composition. This made her a celebrity, especially among people who believed women had talents equal to men and should have the same rights and opportunities as men. Nadia was besieged with requests for interviews. Women composers were still regarded as something freakish, and men in the music community were antagonized every time a woman's name was given top billing at a concert.

Lili, now 16, announced that she wanted to be a composer, and intended to win first prize in the Prix de Rome. But did she have the physical stamina for the intensive study she needed? She progressed rapidly, and only a year-and-a-half later, at age 19, she won the coveted Grand Prix, the first woman to do so for composition. Nadia couldn't help but feel envious that Lili had won the award that had eluded her in spite of her best efforts. She found herself putting distance between herself and Lili, and then feeling guilty. Lili's compositions were being performed at the recitals Madame Boulanger sponsored in her home, and the critics who were invited praised Lili's work. In addition, Lili's fashionable clothes and feminine appearance contrasted with Nadia's, and captured the imagination of the musical public. As an added affront, Nadia was frequently identified as Lili's older sister.

World War I saw many friends of the Boulangers leaving for military service. Nadia and Lili threw themselves into activities to cheer the soldiers who had been musicians and artists. Lili continued to compose. Music teaching all but disappeared, considered unessential at a time when food and shelter were scarce. Lili required more and more of Nadia's time, for nursing care as well as emotional support. In constant pain, Lili's frail body finally succumbed; she died in March 1918 at age 24. Nadia was grief-stricken; from then on, she felt the need to atone for her negative feelings toward her sister. Each year on the anniversary of

Lili's death, she sponsored a commemorative Mass, and for the rest of her life she worked on promoting Lili's compositions.

The United States entered the war, and after it ended, sent war relief supplies to France. Warm feelings developed between the French and American people. An organization called American Friends of Musicians in France had been formed during the war to raise money to support French musicians. The group's president, Walter Damrosch, who was conductor of the New York Symphony, raised the idea of having a music school in France for American musicians. He enlisted the support of General Pershing, commander of the American army. Such a school would show gratitude of the French toward America, and the American students would benefit by exposure to French culture. The school opened in 1921 at Fontainebleau, 36 miles southeast of Paris, with 90 students.

In 1919 Nadia had been appointed to the faculty of another music school in Paris, which required less of its students than the Conservatory. This position, together with her reputation as a pianist and organist and her employment as part-time music critic for a music magazine gave her new prestige in French music circles. Thus Nadia was a logical choice for the faculty of the music school for Americans; she was named professor of harmony. Twice a week she commuted to Fontainebleau in her newly-purchased black automobile.

Nadia made harmony an exciting study. Her students were impressed with her vast knowledge. She believed that America was on the verge of an outpouring of creativity, and she gave her American students the confidence to carry it out. It was through Nadia that American students like Aaron Copland, Virgil Thomson, and Walter Piston met the conductors that helped launch their careers as composers. However, she turned down George Gershwin when he approached her for lessons. "You would only lose the spontaneity of your music," she told him. Nadia took a personal interest in all her students, and became a mother-figure to some, admonishing those who she felt were not eating properly or getting enough sleep. At the age of 35, she was already a living legend.

An opportunity arose for Nadia to tour the U.S. to lecture and perform in 1925. But her lecture-recitals received little notice in the press, and so the impression she made on American music circles was limited. Upon her return to Paris, she found her mother suffering from Parkinson's disease. Again Nadia found herself looking after a family member instead of working on her career.

Among Nadia's students were a number of child prodigies. She was demanding of them, and in return expected total loyalty, for she needed their emotional support as much as they needed her. A great deal of new music was performed in the salons of Paris; the salons were gathering places, usually homes of wealthy families, where persons interested in the arts, literature, or politics could hear new works and discuss new trends. Since the salons were frequented by French aristocrats, Nadia made sure that her students' social graces were such that they could mingle with ease. True to her mother's teachings, she never revealed any negative feelings or emotional vulnerability. When a student took leave to strike out on his own, she grieved privately as though the loss was of a child. A voluminous correspondence helped her stay in touch with former students and friends.

Wednesday afternoons were the time for weekly gatherings at Nadia's apartment when the most modern music was played and analyzed. Sometimes medieval madrigals would be sung. Later, tea and cake were served.

By 1929, Nadia had been teaching for 26 years. Though known chiefly as a teacher of composers, she was also sought out by performers who wished to study interpretation with her. She was known for being able to diagnose instantly a student's weak points, and give him what was needed to improve in that area. Also, she could show a student just how his composition fitted into musical tradition by playing phrases of other works, like a juggler throwing more and more objects into the air. Technique, she believed, "must be mastered to the point where it sets the performer free to interpret the essentials of the music." For her more talented students, she actively promoted their compositions.

By the mid-Thirties, Nadia's former students filled professorships in music departments throughout the U.S., and thereby spread her fame. She had also brought on an innovation in France— talks to introduce young children to the joys of music. "If you train children to distinguish tones and tonalities as you train them to distinguish colors, they would later listen more sensitively to music," she wrote.

In June, 1932, Nadia was awarded the French Legion of Honor. Previously she had been chosen the outstanding French woman in the Arts by the readers of a popular French women's magazine.

Having added conducting and writing music criticism to her activities, Nadia became the first woman to conduct the orchestras of London, New

York, Boston, Philadelphia, and Washington. When asked how it felt to be the first woman to conduct the Boston Symphony, she replied, "Conducting an orchestra is a job. I don't think gender plays much part."

During World War II, when the German army was marching towards Paris, Nadia decided to leave France, though feeling bad about abandoning her country. She had a contract to teach in the U.S. A full schedule of teaching and giving lecture-recitals often left her tired and short-tempered. Her earnings were either sent back to France or offered to the war effort in the States.

In January 1946 Nadia returned to France, having been appointed Professor of Accompaniment at the Paris Conservatory, a post she had waited 23 years for. Soon after, the American Conservatory reopened, with Nadia as head of the composition and theory departments.

In her columns as music critic, Nadia bestowed lavish praise on her composer friends, especially her favorite, Igor Stravinsky. Although Stravinsky's early music had been revolutionary and an object of scorn among music lovers, Nadia recognized its value: "It satisfies one's mental faculties and also touches the heart," she wrote. Those whose music she did not care for she ignored; one of these was

Arnold Schoenberg, whose serialist 12-tone music she did not consider music at all.

Always the teacher, Nadia was eager to help any musician, but her methods were blunt and direct. Once, after a piano recital, she told the artist, "Your Chopin was sloppy. Come and see me at 7 a.m. tomorrow. We will work on the Chopin." A favorite saying of hers was, "It is one thing to be gifted, and another thing to become worthy of one's own gift."

Nadia continued to teach, conduct, and write about music, even though in her seventies her health began to decline. Her eyesight was failing, arthritis limited the use of her hands, and her teeth were bad. She could no longer be in control of every situation, and so she made life miserable for the people around her. Yet she could still look at an orchestral score, sit down at the piano and play it, and understand immediately the music's inner structure.

For her 80th birthday, a gala concert and reception took place in Monaco, attended by Prince Rainier and Princess Grace.

Nadia lived a month past her 92nd birthday. Her uniqueness as a teacher was due to her passionate enthusiasm and intensity, her broad knowledge of music, her critical sense, and her ability to inspire a student. As the music critic of the *New York Times* wrote, "If there is one person who shaped the course of our music from 1920 to 1940, that person is Nadia Boulanger."

Margaret Bourke-White in 1965
(AP/WideWorld Photos)

Margaret Bourke-White, Photographer

Look, Margaret," Joe White said to his eight-year-old daughter, pointing to a bush. "It's the pupa of a butterfly."

"Oh, can we take it home?" Margaret asked eagerly, her dark eyes wide with anticipation. "I want to watch it turn into a butterfly."

"All right. Let me break off the branch. It can go next to the caterpillars on the dining room window sill."

Margaret loved going on walks with her dad through the woods and hills near their New Jersey home. They always came back with something interesting—a jar of frog's eggs, a snake for their terrarium, or a caterpillar that would turn into a small green motionless object and then emerge one day into a wrinkly creature that, when its wings dried, turned into a beautiful butterfly. But, more than their finds, Margaret reveled in the companionship of her father, for Joe White was a quiet man whose thoughts were most often on improving the printing presses that he designed.

He was never satisfied until he knew he had done his absolute best. This was a lesson that Margaret absorbed quite early.

Margaret Bourke-White was born on June 14, 1906, in New York City. Early in her life, Margaret decided that she "would do all the things that women never do." She pictured herself sent to distant places to study the native snakes and turtles. Her family had a few strict rules: no reading of the funnies, and no visiting playmates if their families had comic papers in the house. Movies were seldom allowed, because they were "too easy a form of entertainment for a child", according to Mrs. White.

Margaret did not mind these rules. What hurt her most as a teenager was never being invited to a dance. Other school honors came her way - editing the high school paper and a literary prize - but never a dance invitation, at least not until college.

Margaret was a good student in high school, and entered college in 1924, not knowing what course of study to pursue. After a year of studying art at Columbia, and classes in swimming and esthetic dancing at Rutgers, she enrolled at the University of Michigan to study herpetology. That was where she met, fell in love with, and married

Everett "Chappie" Chapman, a graduate student in electrical engineering.

The couple honeymooned in a lakeside cottage close to the Michigan campus.Chappie's regal, silver-haired mother arrived for an extended visit. Early in the morning, when Chappie had already left for his lab, Margaret heard her mother-in-law's voice from the next room: "Well, Margaret, how did your mother feel when she heard you were going to be married?"

"At first Mother thought we were both too young. But when she saw Chappie and me together and realized we were truly in love, she was glad."

"She's gained a son and I've lost a son." There was a pause. "You got him away from me. I congratulate you. I never want to see you again."

A tearful Margaret left the cottage immediately and walked the 17 miles to the campus to find her husband, thinking he would set things right. But neither of them knew how to deal with this situation. "As a nineteen-year-old wife, I knew a surprising amount about the ways of flying fish and butterflies, but very little of the ways of humans," Margaret wrote. "I had sailed into marriage with the sun in my eyes and the wind in my hair, and when I found myself engulfed in a silver-cord entanglement, I floundered about without a compass."

The two finished the year at Michigan, and moved to Indiana where Chappie would be teaching at Purdue. Margaret enrolled as a student in paleontology, but felt cut off from others because married students were still an oddity, and the wives of other professors were all twice her age.

The couple had to admit that their marriage was a failure, and they separated. But Margaret came out a stronger, more self-confident person, and for that she was grateful to Chappie's mother.

Still bent on studying zoology, Margaret transferred to Cornell, partly because she had read there were waterfalls on the campus. The campus scenery and buildings seemed to call for a photographer to record the scenes. Perhaps students would buy photographs of those scenes, she thought. Margaret liked the feel of a camera in her hands, and by Christmas she had eight or ten pictures that she felt were worthy of being shown. A commercial photographer was helpful in letting her use his darkroom.

The pictures sold well. Several of Margaret's photos were used as covers for the university's Alumni News. Letters came from architects getting the Alumni News, asking if Margaret intended to go into photography after graduation. This presented an attractive new possibility. Should she abandon zoology and concentrate on photography?

She needed unbiased advice. Someone gave her the name of an architectural photographer in New York to go and see. He seemed uninterested until she opened her portfolio and showed him the top photo, a view of the university's library tower. Much impressed, he called in his co-workers to look at her pictures. They agreed that she could walk into any architect's office in the country with that portfolio and get work.

Settling in Cleveland, Margaret made the rounds of architectural firms headed by Cornell alumni or friends of alumni. Her first job was to photograph a new school, for five dollars a picture. After deciding on the angles from which to photograph, she hurried over at dawn on four successive mornings to get the sun where she wanted it, only to give up when the sun refused to come out from an overcast sky. The fifth morning was good, but a few touches of landscaping would improve the pictures. Margaret hurried to a nearby florist, bought an armful of aster plants, and stuck them into the ground around the school. The pictures turned out beautifully, and their publication brought in more work for the fledgling Bourke-White studio. Payment for such pictures, Margaret hoped, would be enough to cover expenses for the experimental photographs she wanted to take.

In the 1920s, the central drama of the country was in industry, the result of a decade of prosperity, and that was what Margaret wanted to record. "The Flats", near downtown Cleveland, was a cluttered area of railroad tracks, the meandering Cuyahoga River, tugboats and barges, smokestacks, brick buildings holding steel mills, and arching bridges carrying traffic overhead. Margaret loved the abstract patterns of railroad trestles, the rounded piles of coal, and the arches of the bridges. Each weekend she raced to the Flats to photograph scenes. She wanted to use her imagination, develop her own style, and make her own mistakes. In a burst of whimsy, she made camera cloths in colors to match her clothes.

Her kitchen sink held the developing trays, and rinsing was done in her bathtub. A kindly camera store owner, Alfred Hall Bemis, scrounged more equipment for her, and became a good friend and adviser. He told her, "You can make a million technicians, but not photographers." What he meant was that a true photographer needs to have an artist's eye.

Margaret's first industrial photograph was used by a bank for the cover of its monthly magazine; it brought her fifty dollars. She then approached the president of the bank with a request. Could he get her inside a steel mill to take photos? He must have wondered why a pretty girl would want to take pictures in a dirty steel mill. Nevertheless he sent her to his friend at the Otis Steel Company. She explained to this man that industry, and especially steel mills, had a power and vitality and drama that made it a fit subject for photography. He agreed to let her inside those brick walls.

Every night for five months, Margaret roamed through the building, exploring, focusing, choosing viewpoints, and having the time of her life.

But the pictures did not turn out well, for there was too much contrast between light and dark to show details. Flashbulbs had not been invented yet. An acquaintance of Mr. Bemis came to Cleveland on his way to Hollywood to demonstrate a new way of lighting scenes using magnesium flares. He came to the steel mill with Bemis and Margaret to help. Of the twelve flares he had with him, eleven were used up in the steel mill. The photos came out better, but the enlargements looked bad. Another traveling salesman came to the rescue with a new kind of paper to make prints.

The steel mill executive liked the photos, purchased eight for $100 each, and asked Margaret to make eight more, all to be used in a book, *The Story of Steel,* for the company's stockholders.

In the spring of 1929, Henry R. Luce, the publisher of *Time* magazine, offered Margaret a job. *Why should they be interested in me,* she wondered; Time *only uses portraits of important persons, and meanwhile there are railroads, factories, docks and bridges all over the country waiting to be photographed by me.*

What Luce planned was a new magazine called *Fortune*, that would show every corner of industry and depend greatly on photographs. A starry-eyed Margaret accepted the job offer.

Her early assignments included photographing shoe factories in Masachusetts, light bulb factories in Corning, New ork, orchid growing in New Jersey, and fisheries in Connecticut. A tour of industries in Indiana with Luce himself taught Margaret that while pictures could be beautiful, they must also present information. In addition to the industrial photos for Luce's magazine, she now turned to advertising photography. This taught her a new technique. Each picture must be convincing; a bowl of soup must look good enough to eat; a rubber tire must look more like rubber than rubber itself. She learned to think in terms of abstract color patterns and composed her pictures accordingly.

With *Fortune* magazine firmly established, Margaret looked for new frontiers to conquer. The country of Russia, just developing its heavy industry in the early Thirties, beckoned. After numerous postponements, Margaret got permission to travel and take pictures. Besides still photos, she also made a movie, which was eventually distributed in the U.S.

The drama of the Great Depression followed the drama of industry. The *Fortune* editors sent Margaret to photograph the results of the great drought of 1934. She was moved by the suffering of the farmers whose crops withered in the blistering sun and whose farm animals choked on windblown soil. For the first time Margaret was aware of people as the subject of photography.

A well-known writer, Erskine Caldwell, chose Margaret to travel with him to record the conditions of tenant farmers. They agreed to start in six months; Margaret first needed to complete other projects. The six months passed quickly, and she was still not ready. She called to ask Caldwell for a one-week postponement. He was very cool, and she feared the whole project was off. There was only one thing to do. She finished up her work in four days and caught a plane to Augusta, Georgia. From her hotel room she sent a written message to

Caldwell, who was staying in a village six miles away. The day dragged on while she waited anxiously for a reply. At six Caldwell himself showed up, and they started on their trip immediately. While Caldwell talked to the southern sharecroppers, Margaret snapped photos of their faces, their modest shacks, and their land. Their joint work became *You Have Seen Their Faces,* a book that was well-received, and took on a life of its own by influencing others, just as *Uncle Tom's Cabin* had influenced people some 85 years before.

In the meantime, Henry Luce launched another new magazine, called *Life*, which was to tell the news through pictures. Margaret felt her horizons widening again. This magazine would interpret human situations from throughout the world. It would "absorb everything we photographers had to give: all the understanding we were capable of, all the speed in working, the imagination, the good luck . . . My cup was running over."

The new magazine sent Margaret all over the world on assignments. Sometimes she presented ideas for photo stories herself, and got permission to carry them out. While on assignment near the Arctic Circle in Canada, a telegram came from

Caldwell: "Come home and marry me."

This was a source of concern for Margaret. Her first loyalty was to her profession. Dashing off at a moment's notice to some far corner of the world was not conducive to a happy marriage. And when concentrating on angles and illuminations for her photos, she did not want to think about Caldwell and his unpredictable moods. But perhaps this man really needed her. Finally she agreed to marry him.

From the late Thirties to 1945, the world's attention shifted to Europe, where World War II was being fought. Margaret and her husband were in Russia when the war broke out. Margaret sent photos of the German bombing raids to *Life*, furnishing the magazine with photographic scoops that tied in with the day's news.

After five years of marriage, Margaret and her husband found that their careers were leading them into separate lives. They parted on friendly terms.

In 1942 Margaret was named by the U.S. Air Force an official war correspondent. As the first woman with this title, a special uniform was designed for her, and for any future women correspondents. On a ship stuffed with British and American troops, Margaret sailed to North Africa. The ship was torpedoed in the Mediterranean, and everyone scrambled into lifeboats. After a day at sea, those in Margaret's lifeboat were rescued by a passing destroyer.

Fighting moved from North Africa to Italy, then to France, and finally to Germany. Margaret divided her time between photographing from reconnaissance planes and photographing artillery crews as they shelled the German positions. When a screech or a whoosh signaled an incoming German shell, everyone dived to the ground, only to resume their work after the inevitable explosion. Descriptions of the action, the soldiers, and the heroic nurses were published along with Margaret's photographs in a book titled *Purple Heart Valley*.

It bothered Margaret that in both Italy and Germany, nothing was done after their defeat to woo them towards democracy. She wrote, "It was not enough to conquer territory if we did not educate it in such a way that we could live at peace with it in the future." The German people seemed to have no remorse over what their leaders had done; they were only sorry that Germany had lost the war.

In the late 40s and 50s, Margaret photographed the people of India, who were about to gain independence from Britain, as well as South African mine workers, and soldiers fighting the Korean War. In addition, she made portraits of many world leaders of that time.

Margaret summed up her work philosophy this way: "In a whole lifetime of taking pictures, a photographer knows that the time will come when he will take one picture that seems the most important of all . . . You hope that the emotion you are trying to capture will be a real one, and will be reflected on the faces of the people you are photographing." Such a picture was one that Margaret took of a Korean mother reunited with the son she thought was dead.

In the late 1950s, Margaret noticed she was having difficulty walking and controlling her hand muscles. She was given exercises to do, but Parkinson's disease is a progressive malady that has no cure, and she quickly became incapacitated. A new medical procedure — an operation on the brain — proved to be Margaret's salvation. After weeks of physical therapy, she learned to walk again. She felt extremely lucky to be able to profit from the advancement of medical science.

Margaret Bourke-White died in 1971. More than anyone else, she raised photography to an art form. She became, through her photography, one of the outstanding personalities on the American scene, and her recording of 'history in the making' secured for her a sure place in history herself.

Beverly Sills in *Manon*,1969
(AP/WideWorld Photos)

Beverly Sills, Opera Star

When Beverly Sills performed for the last time on October 27, 1980, she had been singing for audiences for 47 years. The last thirty years of her career consisted of appearances in opera houses around the world.

Beverly was born May 26, 1929, the only daughter of Morris Silverman, a life insurance salesman, and his wife Shirley. From an early age she was nicknamed Bubbles. The Silvermans were a close-knit family, and Bubbles' two older brothers were protective toward her. Mrs. Silverman filled the house with operatic music from the record player she kept in the kitchen of their Brooklyn, New York, home. Little Bubbles absorbed the music and soon could sing the melodies herself.

When Bubbles was four, her mother took her to audition for a radio show that advertised for "talented children". To get on Bob Emery's show, the children had to attend classes in dancing, elocution, and singing before the show each Saturday. Then "Uncle Bob" would choose which children would be on that day's show. Lively little Bubbles was always among those chosen.

A family friend arranged for Bubbles to sing at the opening of a new restaurant. She was billed as "Beverly Sills". Mr. Silverman was angry about the name change. "Isn't our name Silverman good enough?" he grumbled. But in time he accepted his daughter's stage name.

For four years Bubbles was a regular on Bob Emery's show. By this time she was fluent in French, the result of having a French babysitter. That meant she could sing French songs as easily as English. Mrs. Silverman then took her to audition for Major Bowes' Original Amateur Hour, a popular radio show. Bubbles became a regular on that program, singing operatic arias.

Mr. Silverman was not happy about his daughter's budding singing career. He expected her to become a teacher - the only respectable career for a woman, he thought. But Mrs. Silverman was glad that Bubbles shared her love of opera. She dreamed of Bubbles becoming a great opera star.

At summer camp in New Jersey when Bubbles was ten, she got her first leading role, as Yum-Yum in *The Mikado*. After that, whenever she and her mother attended an opera, Bubbles fancied herself singing that role. She continued singing on the radio for another year. Then she was hired to do the world's first singing commercial, a little jingle about Rinso laundry soap. The writers of a soap opera titled *Our Gal Sunday* wrote in a part for her, which lasted 36 weeks. Then Mr. Silverman put his foot down: no more radio shows. But he did not object to Bubbles' private lessons in piano, singing and languages.

At twelve, Bubbles was a tall, gawky girl, set apart from her classmates by the beautiful hand-tailored clothes that her mother made. Though she spent much time on her singing lessons and playing records of her favorite singers, she still enjoyed playing hopscotch with neighborhood girls. Her mother and her voice teacher, Estelle Liebling, also saw that she read books, mostly the English classics of Dickens and the Bronte sisters.

Miss Liebling, Bubbles wrote, "opened up a whole new world for me." Bubbles and her mother would be invited to dinner, and be surrounded by famous opera singers. After dinner, Miss Liebling would have Bubbles sing a song or two for the assembled guests. The dinners always included Bubbles' favorite dish, a souffle.

Miss Liebling took Bubbles to sing for J. J. Shubert, a Broadway producer, who offered her a job as understudy for the female lead of the show he was then producing. She was 15 then, no longer gawky, but an attractive blonde. After that show closed, Shubert offered her a contract to go touring, singing in Gilbert and Sullivan operettas.

"I don't want her to go!" Mr. Silverman declared.

"But this is a wonderful opportunity for her," Mrs. Silverman responded. "You know how much she loves to sing. And she's quite mature for her age. I'm sure she won't do anything foolish."

Mrs. Silverman won him over. A girl in the cast agreed to act as Bubbles' chaperone. One of the chaperone's jobs was to use a special color rinse on Bubbles' hair; she got the formula wrong, and Bubbles turned into a redhead. She remained a redhead ever since.

The touring company performed six nights a week. Bubbles learned a great deal about stagecraft, and toned down her Brooklyn accent for her stage roles. Stage fright was something she never experienced. While on tour, she completed the Professional Children's School courses by correspondence.

Back in Brooklyn, Bubbles began studying opera roles in earnest, through singing lessons three times a week. By the time she was 19, she had memorized all the roles to 50 or 60 operas.

"You must understand the words you are singing, and sing them like you really mean them,"

Miss Liebling said. "I am going to send you to another teacher who is an expert in Italian opera." So every Saturday Bubbles took the train to Philadelphia for a special lesson. This teacher got her a big break, singing the role of Frasquita in the Philadelphia Civic Opera's production of *Carmen*. Now she was no longer just a student, but a real opera singer.

Mr. Silverman's death from cancer in 1949 left Bubbles as well her mother depressed. But a scholarship to study with the well-known singer Mary Garden lifted her depression. Miss Garden taught her every gesture to make while singing in the operas *Manon* and *Thais*. Then, admittance to a special class in France sent Bubbles and her mother sailing to Europe. The classes were held on the stage of the Paris Opera. Bubbles wondered how soon she would sing there for an actual performance.

Miss Liebling arranged an audition for Bubbles with an opera touring company. The organizer, Charles Wagner, told her, "Miss Sills, you are going to be a star!" At the end of that tour, she wrote of her role in the opera *La Traviata,* "I could sing Violetta standing on my head or doing somersaults."

The next few years found Bubbles singing in

Baltimore, San Francisco, and Salt Lake City, and on a television show called "Opera Cameos." In the spring of 1953 she auditioned for the New York City Opera and was hired. She was to sing with this company for 27 years.

In 1954, while singing in Cleveland, Bubbles met the man she was to marry, Peter Greenough, an editor with the Cleveland newspaper *The Plain Dealer*. They decided to get married as soon as his divorce became final. Neither of their families was overjoyed about the marriage. He was twelve years older and already had three children; she was Jewish, he was not. Nevertheless, they were married on November 17, 1956.

Peter's friends and associates did not accept Beverly. On many occasions she felt the sting of prejudice. The final straw was a party; of 40 people invited to the Greenough home, only one couple showed up.

"Why are they so mean to us?" Beverly sobbed later. "Can't we live somewhere besides Cleveland?"

She did some serious thinking. Did she really want to be an opera star? She was then singing at the New York City Opera three weeks in the spring, one month in the fall, and summers at Cleveland's

Musicarnival. But singing was too much a part of her to give it up.

A new opera was to be produced at the New York City Opera titled *The Ballad of Baby Doe*. Many sopranos had already auditioned for the leading role, but none had been chosen. Beverly at 5'8" was told she was too tall for the part; Baby Doe was supposed to be a cute, kittenish kind of girl. Nevertheless, she was asked to audition for the composer, Douglas Moore. "Too tall, am I?" she thought. "I'll show them what tall really is." She came to the audition in spike heels, wearing a huge hat. Size notwithstanding, she got the part. She had six weeks to prepare for the role. Opening night went perfectly, and the newspaper reviews were ecstatic. The *New York Herald Tribune* even put its review on the front page! This role was a major triumph in Beverly's career. The opera was performed in four of the next five seasons.

Beverly was overjoyed when she discovered she was pregnant. Meredith Holden Greenough was born in Cleveland on August 4, 1959. However, the infant had yellow jaundice and hyaline membrane disease, which meant she had trouble breathing. Muffy, as she was called, responded to eight days of treatment in the hospital and went home with her happy mother.

The Cleveland newspaper was sold, and Peter got a share of the price, making him a multimillionaire. A new job awaited him on the staff of a Boston newspaper. So Beverly's five bitter years in Cleveland came to an end.

In Boston, the conductor Sarah Caldwell had started her own opera company. Miss Caldwell asked Beverly to sing in her production of *Die Fledermaus*, but she had to decline because she was pregnant again. Peter Greenough Junior was born June 29, 1961.

Muffy, now two years old, was not talking. A visit to a specialist gave the parents the news that she had a hearing loss. She was fitted with a hearing aid, which she kept hiding, thinking this was a wonderful game.

When the new baby, nicknamed Bucky, failed to respond to anyone or anything around him, he was diagnosed as being autistic. As he got older, he became hyperactive and given to injuring himself.

Beverly was overwhelmed by her children's handicaps. She stayed at home, crushed and unable to face the world. How ironic that the daughter of an opera singer would never be able to hear her mother's beautiful voice!

Beverly's mother flew to Boston frequently to help out. She talked to Muffy for hours on end, even though she knew Muffy could not hear her. She insisted that Muffy have art and dance lessons. In due time, Muffy learned to lip-read and to speak.

Beverly returned to opera, singing in Sarah Caldwell's production of *Manon*, and new productions in New York. Whereas performing on an operatic stage had always been sheer delight for her, now it was pleasant because for three hours she could forget her troubles at home and become someone else. Over the next few years. Beverly sang in about 20 operas for Miss Caldwell. Her *Manon* led to engagements all over the world.

Even when she had the flu, Beverly hated to cancel a scheduled performance. She felt "even if I had to be carried on stage feet first, I should sing... though a little bit less than at full potential, I still deliver a first-class performance."

In 1966 both the New York City Opera and the Metropolitan Opera moved into a new complex called Lincoln Center. Music critics and other writers came to report on the Metropolitan's new home. They were not impressed by the Met's opening production, but they raved about the City Opera's *Julius Caesar* by the Baroque composer G. F. Handel, and especially about Beverly's performance as *Cleopatra*.

Cleopatra was a role that Beverly had wanted

badly to sing. When it was first offered to another singer from the Metropolitan Opera Company, Beverly threatened to quit the City Opera. "Going outside the company to find another soprano was a public admission that nobody in the house could sing that role," she told the director, Julius Rudel. "How about me?" The critics' praises proved that she was the right choice.

An offer came to sing at Italy's La Scala, the Cadillac of opera houses. Beverly was to substitute for a soprano who was a great favorite of Italian audiences. The costume made for this soprano did not fit Beverly, and the costume seamstress refused to alter it. In front of the entire cast, Beverly took a pair of scissors and cut the costume in half. After that, the backstage staff was more cooperative. More offers poured in for Beverly after her La Scala performance.

She was now 40 years old, and faced with decisions. Should she stick to safe, easy roles, or try new challenging ones? She had always figured on retiring at fifty, so she had ten years of singing still ahead. A challenging role came her way in Donizetti's opera *Roberto Devereux*, which was about England's Queen Elizabeth I and the Earl of Essex. This was probably the finest achievement of her career. After a particularly fine performance,

Beverly would think, "Miss Liebling would have liked that." Her beloved teacher had died in September 1970 at age 91.

Whereas before, Beverly had sung for the approval of the public and the critics; now she sang for pure pleasure, "from the real satisfaction from what I have given of myself." She always made the most of dramatic moments in the operas; sometimes the music and the drama of the story moved both her and her co-stars to tears. If she felt emotionally drained when the curtain came down, she considered the performance a success.

A magazine story in 1971 called Beverly "The Fastest Voice Alive," referring not only to her vocal ability, but also to the fact that she could learn a part almost overnight.

A superstar now, Beverly was in demand for TV talk shows. She agreed to them because they helped popularize opera. By the 1970s, opera was being performed in almost every town in the U.S., not only in New York, Chicago, and the west coast. The oil barons of Texas needed to find a place to spend their money, so they poured it into the arts. New opera houses sprang up in Houston, San Antonio, and other Sun Belt cities.

The Greenoughs decided that Bucky needed to be cared for in an institution, which they did reluctantly. Muffy progressed in her lessons and showed artistic talent. In 1972 Beverly was asked to become national chairman of the Mothers' March for Birth Defects. In this role, she and Muffy traveled around the country making speeches and appearing on public radio and TV. She was proud to have helped raise more than fifty million dollars, "as satisfying as anything I have done in my opera career."

In 1975 Beverly was asked to sing at the Metropolitan. Her debut opera was Rossini's *The Siege of Corinth.* Although she had already proved that one could become an international opera star without the "Met", it was gratifying to sing there.

In 1977, Beverly began easing into what would become a second career for her. Julius Rudel, conductor and general manager of the New York City Opera for 21 years, wanted to devote himself to conducting. Beverly agreed to become his co-manager. But then Rudel left to take a post in Buffalo, and Beverly found herself managing an opera company that was in bad financial shape. She raised money from foundations, company heads, and ordinary donors. At times she felt she was trying to revive a corpse. People expected her to fall on her face; whoever heard of a woman running an opera company? That gave her even more reason to keep the company alive.

The pressure of fund-raising left no time to feel bad about the end of a singing career. But audiences that used to come to hear Beverly sing now stayed away. Frantically, Beverly raised ticket prices, then cut them again. She asked the whole company to accept a wage freeze, and she got the mayor of New York to increase the city's financial support. She canceled the spring season in order to lengthen the fall season. Then she introduced an innovation — subtitles above the stage. Audiences loved them; now they could understand each line and laugh at the right places. Other opera companies adopted the practice. Gradually the City Opera moved from the brink of bankruptcy to the brink of success.

Looking back on an illustrious career, Beverly Sills can be proud that she did much to popularize opera in America, both through her singing and then her astute management of one of the leading opera companies of the country. Her Doctor of Music citation from Harvard University reads, "Her joyous personality, glorious voice, and deep knowledge of music and drama bring delight to her audiences and distinction to her art."

Still active in the musical world, Beverly is at present (early 1998) chairman of the board of Lincoln Center in New York City.

Mary Cassatt
(From a painting by Degas)

Mary Cassatt, Painter

By the time Mary Cassatt was sixteen, she knew that she wanted to study art and become an artist. It was fashionable in the mid-nineteenth century for young ladies in the United States to study art, because some knowledge and ability in that field was considered a social accomplishment, something that made a girl more desirable to young men. But Mary wanted more than that; she wanted to become a real artist who paints for a living.

Her father was appalled! No daughter of his was going to actually paint for a living!

Mary was born May 22, 1844, in Pittsburgh, the youngest of five surviving children of a well-off, middle-class family. Her father Robert S. Cassatt was a real estate agent, and both parents were knowledgeable in literature and art. The family moved to Philadelphia when Mary was five, and two years later, they went to Europe for an extended stay. In Paris, Mary's world consisted of walks in public gardens, where she met other children with their nannies, indoor games with her sisters, and trips to museums with her parents. After two years in Paris, the family moved to Heidelberg in

Germany, then back to Paris, and finally back to Philadelphia in 1855, where Mr. Cassatt again took up the business of buying and selling plots of land. All these moves were made "for the benefit of the children," although a good education was considered important only for the Cassatt boys.

In Paris, the Cassatt family visited the World's Fair , which contained a large collection of art objects from all over the world. Mary gazed at each painting in admiration. Some day she would paint pictures too, she told herself—not those kinds of pictures, but beautiful pictures nevertheless.

The United States of 1860 was in a turmoil over the slavery question. Southern leaders were calling for secession of the southern states. It was a dangerous time to be traveling, Mr. Cassatt told Mary, but if she was determined to study art, he would allow her to enroll at the Pennsylvania Academy of Fine Arts, which she could attend while living at home.

So Mary became one of the young ladies copying paintings and sketching statues at the Academy. The only art school in Philadelphia, it had 300 to 400 students, the majority of them girls. The classes were meant to train the students how to draw accurately and in perspective, and how to use paint, charcoal, and pastels. Inspiration was something they would have to find within themselves later. Mary proved to be more gifted and less frivolous than the other students, but she felt she was not learning much. However, she remained for four years, knowing that if she was to progress, she must go to Europe.

It took two years for Mary to break down her father's resistance, but at last, in 1866, she left for Paris. She was accompanied by her mother and sister, who remained with her to act as chaperones, even though Mary was almost 22. Her first teacher, a Mr. Chaplin, had her copy paintings and imitate his style. Although Mary was not sure what kind of painting she wanted to do, she knew it was not the kind Mr. Chaplin did.

Knowing that many of the old masters in the art field were Italian, she went to Italy to study their paintings. For hours she stood in front of a Da Vinci painting or a Correggio, taking in their use of color, their placement of figures in the painting, their choice of subjects to paint, and their treatment of background. She was enchanted with the gleaming figures of Correggio and his lifelike little angels frolicking above. While staying in the Italian city of Parma, she exhibited a painting that, according to a friend's report, "all Parma is flocking to see . . .

Italian painters are quite enthusiastic and offer her every inducement to make Parma her home."

In 1872 Mary got up enough courage to submit a painting to the Salon of Paris. The Salon was an annual exhibit of paintings, and only the best ones were accepted. Eagerly she awaited news from the Salon committee. What a thrill it was when her painting titled "During the Carnival" was accepted! Now she could write to her father that the money he had spent on her was not wasted. But she still had so much to learn.

Next she traveled to Spain, Belgium, and Holland to study the paintings hanging in their museums, pictures by the artists Rubens, Hals, and others. The following year the Salon accepted another of her paintings, this one of a young girl and a bullfighter.

After Mary's father retired, both parents and her sister moved to Paris. Now Mary led two separate lives, a French one with her artist friends, and an American one with her family. She had always preferred men as friends, the result of her easy relationship with her brothers. Most of her friends were male artists. But, still chaperoned, she could not go to the cafes where struggling young artists met to talk endlessly about art.

Mary's brother Alexander had a successful

career in the U.S. and sent them money so that they could rent a villa outside Paris for vacations. There in the tranquil countryside, Mary could paint to her heart's content. Mary knew of the work of a number of fellow artists, especially that of Edgar Degas. She often went to the gallery where Degas' paintings were on display. "I used to go and flatten my nose against the window," she wrote, "and absorb all I could of his art. It changed my life. I saw art then as I wanted to see it." Degas, on his part, was impressed with Mary's work, especially her third painting to be accepted by the Salon. He told a friend "Here is someone who feels as I do." It was inevitable that the two became friends. Whether there was ever any romance between them, no one knows.

Although Degas was an admirer, he could be quite mean. He would say encouraging things and then take them away with a nasty comment. Several times he and Mary had a falling-out, but since they frequented the same exhibits and restaurants, they would sooner or later meet and then be friends again.

Degas and some of the other young artists painted in a new style. They painted ordinary people and street scenes, not queens and heroic warriors, or saints and gods and goddesses. The

Salon would not accept any of their paintings, so a group of them held their own exhibit. But the public didn't like their art either.

"That one looks as though the painter filled a pistol with paint and fired it at the canvas," said one man. "What a laughable collection of absurdities!" said another. One critic gave the entire group a name, meant to be sarcastic: Impressionism. The name stuck. "The Impressionists" came to mean artists that were fascinated with the way light and shadow fell on water, fields, flowers, and people's faces. Except for Degas, they painted in the open, never indoors. They rejected the dark somber colors used in the past. Their colors were bright and vibrant, and they saw beauty in the most everyday scenes.

Their noncomfomity angered the people running the Salon. These Impressionists are ruining art, they complained. They are dangerous, like persons plotting a revolution! But although they caused an uproar in art circles, at least they were no longer unknown. Everyone was talking about them!

When Alexander came to Paris for a long visit, Mary took him to a number of art galleries. He was not particularly interested in art, but Mary persuaded him to buy several paintings by her friends Pissarro and Monet. "In a few years their value will be much greater, and you'll be glad to have them," she told him.

With frequent visits from nieces and nephews, Mary turned more and more to painting children. "It's true that they wiggle and squirm while sitting for me" she explained, "but they don't complain about how they look in the completed painting, as so many adults do."

In 1877 Mary was asked to exhibit her paintings with the Impressionists. "I agreed gladly," Mary related to a friend. "At last I could work absolutely independently without worrying about the possible opinion of a jury. I had already acknowledged who my true masters were. I admired Manet, Courbet, and Degas. I hated conventional art."

At this exhibit Mary met and became friends with a woman artist named Berthe Morisot. The two were often compared as artists, but they were not jealous of each other; their styles were too different.

At Mary's suggestion, the American Art Association invited a French art dealer named Mr. Ruel to organize an exhibit of Impressionist paintings in New York. Some of the artists objected. "I would be sorry to see some of my paintings go to Yankeeland," grumbled Monet, who was to become famous soon after. "Paris is the only place where there is still good taste."

The exhibit took place in April 1886 with about 300 paintings. Mary was represented by two paintings, loaned by Alexander. Many of the paintings were sold. The newspapers mentioned that Mary Cassatt was the driving force behind the exhibit, and she was given credit for introducing America to the art of the French painters.

One of Mary's greatest pleasures and way of relaxation was horseback riding. She often rode through the public parks and stopped to visit this or that friend. In the summer of 1888 she fell from her horse, broke her leg and dislocated her shoulder. "A stupid accident," she told her friends. "It never should have happened." From then on, she never rode again.

Mary's close friend Louisine Elder was a teenager when they first met, and later, an avid art collector. Mary squired young Louisine around Paris, opening her eyes to the beauty to be found in art salons and on the stage. In her memoirs, Louisine wrote: "Miss Cassatt was the most intelligent woman I had ever met, and I cherished every word she uttered. . . Only the dullest mind could fail to retain her original and suggestive remarks, for they stuck like burrs in one's memory and pricked the imagination for many years to come."

One of Mary's good friends was the Impressionist painter Renoir. "I adore the brown tones in your shadows," she told him. "Tell me how you do it." "When you learn to pronounce your r's," he responded, teasing Mary over her American-accented French. Another friend, Pissarro, had difficulty supporting his wife and five children from his painting. In order to help, Mary sent him her American friends who wanted to take art lessons. But instead of charging them, he gave the Americans all the free advice they wanted. Singularly devoted to her art, Mary had no patience for casual visitors. "I have the right to refuse anyone, for I work eight to ten hours a day," she said.

Yet she did entertain occasionally, opening her home to people she found interesting—diplomats, writers, critics, and of course painters.

A showing of Japanese art in Paris got Mary interested in making color prints. These are made by etching a picture on a copper plate with a diamond-tipped needle. There is no way to correct mistakes, but Mary did her etching without any preliminary drawing. She turned out numerous color prints that show the Japanese influence in their lines and use of color. They are considered excellent examples of this technique. If she had never done anything else, these prints give Mary Cassatt a claim to fame.

By this time Mary had so many pictures, she needed a large home to display them. She found an old castle near Paris and purchased it. But it took two years to make it fit to live in. In the meantime Mary's father died. Now Mary and her mother were alone in France. They moved into the castle in 1893, along with a cook, three maids, three gardeners, and a coachman. On the walls Mary hung pictures she had acquired from fellow artists. On the porch walls she hung her Japanese prints.

Two years after moving in, Mary's mother died. Now, after 18 years of having family members around, Mary was on her own.

In 1898 Mary returned to the U.S., her first time in 30 years. But it was with mixed feelings. She felt America had let her down by not recognizing her as a great artist. She longed for one favorable review of her work in America. Although many Americans had come to see her on their trips abroad, and some had bought her paintings, no pictures had been bought by museums.

America had of course changed in thirty years. McKinley was president, there were more buildings, more industry, but also more poverty. Mary's brother Alexander was now president of the Pennsylvania Railroad and one of the most powerful men in American industry. But the people of Philadelphia hardly took notice of her. To them she was simply Alexander's sister. It saddened her that her family cared so little about art. The pictures she had talked Alexander into buying were hung in a dark corner. To her nieces and nephews she was "Aunt Mary who paints and for some reason chose to live in France." Although she never broke with her family, she was hurt. By the end of 1900, she was back in France.

The French art dealers loved Mary because she brought her wealthy American friends to them to buy art. American millionaires routinely bought European art, not because they loved beautiful pictures, but because it was something they felt they should do. But most of them did not have someone like Mary to advise them. The French complained that Americans were taking away their Impressionist paintings, forgetting that they had originally rejected them. Mary's wish was that every home could have works of art on its walls. "Nothing will inspire a taste for art more than the possibility of having it in the home. I should like to feel that amateurs in America could have an example of my work, a print or an etching, for a few dollars . . . In France, it is not left to the rich alone to buy art."

Mary's eyesight began to fail in the early 1900s, but she kept on painting. Slowly her reputation spread in the U.S. The Pennsylvania Academy of Fine Arts awarded her a prize for a painting titled "Caress" but she declined it, saying she didn't believe in medals and awards. However, later, when the same Academy awarded her its Gold Medal of Honor, she accepted it because it was in recognition of her entire work, not for any single painting, and because there was no money involved. She also accepted France's Legion of Honor, an award that was rarely offered to a foreigner or to a woman. This award did much to increase her reputation.

Mary Cassatt died in June 1926, leaving 940 paintings and 224 prints. Almost every large museum in the world has some of her art today, and one of her mother and child paintings hangs in the White House. She was also honored by having her face on a U.S. postage stamp. Gardner Teall, an American painter and illustrator, wrote: "The art of Mary Cassatt is great art because it is the work of a true and gifted humanist who perfectly expresses her humanism." She was truly America's first lady of art.

Julia Morgan
(Special Collections, California Polytechnic State University)

Julia Morgan, Architect

Oakland, California, the Morgans' home town, had grown rapidly, along with its sister city across the bay, San Francisco. Ever since the gold rush of 1849, people kept pouring into California, hoping to make their fortune in mining or ranching or lumber. Bill and Eliza Morgan were among those who had come from New York City and settled in Oakland. Bill Morgan tried various businesses and finally became quite successful as a partner in a company that made steam-powered tractors. Eliza came from a wealthy New York family that provided her with an income of her own.

Julia Morgan was born on January 26, 1872, the oldest girl and second child of Bill and Eliza. Mr. Morgan built a large house at the edge of town for his growing family. Young Julia liked to sit in the bay windows and look at the recently planted elm trees along the street of packed earth. Beyond the last houses, grassy hills rose, green during the rainy winter, and golden-tan during the dry summer. Servants made life comfortable for the Morgans.

Their summers were spent at the Southern California seashore.

Like her mother, Julia was quiet and shy, but willful and at times obstinate. She looked frail, but thanks to her brothers' gym equipment and her practice of archery, she developed strength and stamina. At school, she always ran around with the boys and ignored the girls. But as she grew older, she gave up her tomboy ways and concentrated on her school work. Her mother encouraged her to finish high school, at a time when most girls did not. Girls from poorer families had to help out at home, or go to work in factories. But both Mr. and Mrs. Morgan believed strongly in a good education for all their children. Julia enjoyed her studies, which included Latin and German, at Oakland High School; her favorite subjects were math and science. In addition, she took dancing lessons, and played the piano and violin quite well.

The 1870s and 1880s were an exciting time to be alive in the United States. During this period, the telephone, typewriter, and phonograph were all invented. Electricity came into homes and lit up the streets at night. In 1885 the first modern skyscraper was built. On one of her family's frequent trips to the east coast, Julia saw the Brooklyn Bridge, a marvel of the age, as it was being built. New buildings sprang up like mushrooms in the western cities. People had a deep faith in technology and the progress of science. There seemed to be no limit to future possibilities.

Observing all this change, Julia tried to plan her future while still in her last year of high school. Other girls of her age and class most probably would be debutantes—a way of being presented formally to society in order to show that they were ready to meet eligible young men—but Julia resisted becoming part of this social life. She had never enjoyed parties. What she wanted was to go to college, as more and more girls were doing, and prepare for a career. What kind of career she didn't know; maybe medicine, or maybe music. Mrs. Morgan believed her daughter would be successful at anything she attempted.

The University of California had a branch in Berkeley, close enough to Oakland that Julia could live at home. So it was decided that Julia would enroll at the university there.

Julia had often visited her cousin Lucy, who had married an architect named Pierre LeBrun. She had seen Pierre's drawings of buildings and was impressed by his work. Designing must be challenging, she thought, like the complicated math problems that she loved to solve. Pierre encouraged her interest in math and her talent in drawing, and they began to write to each other frequently. She decided that architecture was what she would study. But had there ever been a woman architect? Mr. and Mrs. Morgan shook their heads in wonder when she told them her plan. But of course they would support her, whatever her goal might be. Since Berkeley did not have courses in architecture, she took the next best thing, civil engineering. She learned how to design roads and bridges, what materials are best for each purpose, how to make drawings of buildings, and how to calculate the allowable loads on beams and columns.

At first Julia was nervous as the horse-drawn streetcar took her from her house to the Berkeley campus. She was glad that her brother Avery accompanied her. Soon, as she fell into a routine of classes and homework, she began enjoying herself, even though her male classmates glared at her and made rude remarks. She felt fortunate that her family's wealth allowed her to go to college.

During her college years, a competition was announced, open to women only, to design a Women's Building for the World's Fair to be held in Chicago in 1893. It was won by a young woman named Sophia Hayden, who was only four years older than Julia. If she can do that, Julia thought,

I'm sure I can do something similar in the future.

One of her professors, impressed by her work, suggested that she get additional training at a famous French school, the Ecole des Beaux-Arts. He had heard that the school was prepared to accept women very soon.

This would be a big step for Julia. She would have to travel across the United States by train, then spend ten or twelve days on a ship crossing the Atlantic. Arriving in Paris, she would have to find a place to live, learn the French language, and study for the school's difficult entrance exams. It was a tremendous challenge, but Julia was determined to succeed.

She was 24 the summer of 1896 when she and a girl cousin sailed to France. The cousin and her professor's French friends helped her to find a furnished apartment.

The Ecole offered entrance exams twice a year for several hundred hopeful architects. Of these, 40 or 50 might pass. To prepare for the exam, the students worked in studios run by individual architects. Julia joined one having about ten students. As a newcomer, she had to complete the older students' projects, adding detail to their drawings. Though she felt her work was adequate, the other students did not take her seriously. Even one of the teachers, "although very kind," she wrote to Pierre, "always seems astonished if I do anything showing the least intelligence, as though that was the last thing expected."

Gradually her command of French improved. She wrote to her parents every week, but never mentioned that she was homesick.

In October 1897, Julia took the exam. Accustomed to dealing with measurement in terms of feet and inches, she could not think in meters. She did not pass this first exam, but tried again the following April. Again she did not pass. Her studio director told her that the examiners had graded her very strictly, as though they did not wish her to pass.

But Julia was stubborn. She studied harder, in spite of developing eye trouble from the strain. She joined another studio, whose director encouraged her. The following October she took the exam for the third time—and passed, ranking 13th out of 40. At last she would have a chance to learn what she needed to know to have a successful career!

Now the real work began. Every month the Ecole gave students a design problem that required detailed drawings. Each student climbed up to the 3rd or 4th floor to a cubbyhole furnished with a drawing board, to complete the work within twelve hours.

Julia finally began to get recognition for her talent. She earned four medals for excellence in design and drawing. She even got some paying work from the outside. Her summers were spent traveling around Europe and sketching old houses and churches. At last, after three years at the Ecole, she graduated as the first woman architect from what was then the best architectural school in the world.

Back in San Francisco, Julia joined an architectural firm that had been hired to design new buildings for the Berkeley campus. But, as had happened at the Ecole, she faced a constant struggle simply because she was a woman. She realized she had to work on her own, so she set up an "office" in the carriage house of her family's home. Soon old friends from college asked her to design homes for them. Other jobs followed—designing a bell tower, a library, and churches. One of her biggest early jobs was rebuilding the Fairmont Hotel, damaged in the disastrous San Francisco earthquake of 1906. Many of the walls in the six-floor building had buckled, and some floors had settled seven feet below where they should be. Julia's experience with reinforced concrete and her engineering training

enabled her to plan and supervise the recon-
struction, so that exactly one year after the
earthquake, the hotel was ready for guests. This
established her reputation.

In approaching a job, Julia first decided on the
inside plan: how large the rooms should be, how
they should be laid out, how high the ceilings
should be, and how much light should come from
the windows. Her designs drew from the traditions
of the American West - the Spanish missions and
Indian pueblos - as well as the European tradition.
Also, she made her buildings blend in with the land
on which they sat.

Besides her family, Julia had no private life.
Her work took up all of her time; her office staff
constituted an extended family. She always hoped
that the young women that she preferred to hire
would share her own dedication, but, as she
complained, "they would go off and get married or
something, and be a disappointment.'

From 1919 on, for the next 25 years, Julia was
kept busy with her biggest job, and the one she is
most remembered for - designing and supervising
the building of a castle on the California coast, near
the village of San Simeon, for William Randolph
Hearst, a publisher who owned many newspapers
and magazines. Hearst was a man who was used to

having his way. This made him difficult to work with, but he and Julia admired each other and could resolve their disagreements.

Work on the castle progressed very slowly. It depended on the weather and on the money that Hearst could pour into it. Most Fridays Julia traveled by night train from San Francisco to the closest town and then took a taxi the rest of the way. She spent Saturday and Sunday supervising the work being done, and returned home Sunday night. The workmen marveled at the tiny, frail-looking woman who was not afraid to climb up flimsy ladders to inspect their work. If Hearst was not there, she would write him a report on the progress. Besides the castle itself, she also had to design three guest houses for Hearst's frequent visitors, two swimming pools, temporary housing for the workers, and enclosures for Hearst's private zoo.

The completed castle has 92 rooms, which include a banquet hall, music room, library, billiard room, ballroom, and servants' quarters. It is now a museum, a fantastic showplace that is noted for its beauty and for the priceless art objects that Hearst collected.

Hearst asked Julia to design other buildings for

him, for he owned land and houses in several places. On a tract of pine-forested land in northern California, she built three storybook-like houses, which Hearst named Sleeping Beauty House, Cinderella House, and Bear House. In the 1930s, a bad ear infection led to dizzy spells for Julia. Hearst sent her to Europe for a long vacation at his expense. But her energy was running low, and she could no longer keep up her normal pace of work. Architectural styles changed in the 1940s; people now wanted clean lines with chrome and steel used in construction, and so they turned to other architects.

When Julia realized her memory was failing, she knew the time had come to give up her practice. Her final years were spent traveling with her niece Flora. She died February 2, 1957, at age 85. Julia Morgan never sought wealth, fame, or publicity. In her long career, she designed more than 700 buildings. She let them speak for her.

Selected Bibliography

Anderson, Marian. *My Lord, What A Morning.* New York: Viking Press, 1956.

Bourke-White, Margaret. *Portriat of Myself.* New York, 1965.

Cain, Michael. *Mary Cassatt.* New York: Chelsea House, 1989.

James, Cary. *Julia Morgan: Architrect.* New York: Chelsea House, 1990.

Monsaingeon, Bruno. *Mademoiselle: Conversations with Nadia Boulanger.* Manchester: Carcanet Press Ltd., 1985.

Sills, Beverly. *Bubbles, A Self-Portriat.* New York: Bobbs-Merrill, 1976.

Tallchief, Maria, with Lary Kaplan. *Maria Tallchief: America's Prima Ballerina.* New York: Henry Holt & Co., 1997.

Index